A Hum

Approach

Subtitle

Balancing Innovation and Ethical Considerations

PAIGB BRONK

1991

ACKNOWLEDGEMENTS

This study has been completed with the help of numerous people. I wish to thank the many people that inspired and helped me to complete the project.

I would like to give a special thank you to Dr. Farhad Atash for lending his support with the project and more. He has been a superb "coach" through the process who contributes a significant amount of patronage by always willing to listen, understand, and lend excellent recommendations. I also would like to express to Kathy Maxwell how deeply appreciative I am of the information and suggestions she has given to me. She has been an imperative resource in respect to the overall quality of the study.

The Community Planning Class of 1991 has always inspired me to push forward and to keep going. I intend to hold on to this philosophy and use it forever after leaving the program. Also, a special thanks to Dr. John Kupa for lending his expertise and knowledge from which I have learned lots over the past years.

TABLE OF CONTENTS

LIST OF FIGURES

FIGURES

LIST OF APPENDICES

APPENDICES

DEDICATED TO MY BELATED FRIEND, HAPPY.

CHAPTER ONE

CHAPTER 1

SOLID WASTE DILEMNA AND SCOPE OF STUDY

I. Introduction/Problem Statement

Solid waste disposal and management has steadily become one of the largest municipal dilemnas of the 1990's. Communities within the United States have been disposing of most of their municipal wastes through the relatively simple method of landfilling. This method was at one time quite economically feasible and extremely simple. The present day problem with this crude strategy arises due to the lack of finite land resources, increased regulations, and larger quantities of waste.

Our nation generates approximately 160 million tons of garbage annually. [1] "Despite widespread recognition that 80 percent of the landfills now in operation will reach capacity and close within 20 years, only a handful of new landfills have been approved." [2] The problem is that communities will not be able to rely soley on the landfill approach for the disposal of their solid waste. Alternative means must be devised, planned for, implemented, and managed.

Communities, states, and regions have already tackled this growing problem by devising what is commonly called the "Integrated Approach". According to the Environmental Protection Agency, this approach attempts to incorporate waste processes and technologies together in the following hierarchical order: waste reduction, recycling, composting, incineration and landfilling.[3]

The recycling element is one of the largest growing elements of the approach in terms of popularity and community implementation. "Recycling is essentially an activity involving the transformation of a post-consumer material discard into a new, reformulated product. This transformation process includes the collection of the discards, primarily through separation at curbside; delivery of the separated materials to recycling centers or recovery as mixed waste at a separate facility; the sale of those materials often through a broker, as raw materials; the crushing, grinding, or other ways of reformulating the material for production; the development of a new product; and its marketing to various users, some of which could be accomplished through government procurement programs." [4] This process captures waste at the source before waste reaches landfills and incinerators. Recycling allows materials to be reused, thereby reducing the actual volume of waste entering landfills and incinerators. This reduction will not only add longevity to our landfills and incinerators, but will conserve land, water, and air resources.

The question for investigation is, why should other communities also turn more to the recycling element and how can they approach the implementation of this component in a planned and effective way? While communities within Rhode

Island have implemented programs due to state recycling mandates, other communities nationwide have not even begun to consider the option.

There have been many articles and books that have analyzed particular aspects of recycling, but apparently few have attempted to provide a generic but comprehensive description of guidelines and points of interest for the community interested in investigating the implementation of a recycling program. The importance of this particular project lies in the focus of implementation guidelines for a recycling program. Documentation establishing a starting-point for communities stating possible needs for consideration and caution towards potential problems is extremely important. Comprehensive guidance towards solving community dilemnas such as the solid waste disposal problem is especially beneficial during hardened economic situations as is the case in 1991.

II. Objectives of the Study

The main objectives of the study encompass generic but specific focal points in regard to the implementation of a curbside recycling program. There are six chapters which attempt to analyze all important considerations a waste manager and community may have in respect to implementation. These chapters do not attempt to press communities towards using any one recommendation unless experts from various sources unanimously agree with the recommendation. The purpose of the chapters is to simply illustrate several different points of interest and consideration for the community. Decisions as to which specific approaches a curbside recycling program should take can not usually be determined by duplicating the templates of other community programs. Every community differs in respect to its individual parameters, and every community will have a different recycling model that will be the most efficient for that given area.

Chapter two explains the basic history and philosophy of the solid waste situation and recycling. The chapter also comments about the integrated approach along with an analysis of comparing high technological solid waste solutions to the more low technological recycling approach. Within this chapter the "New Effeciency" philosophy is discussed.

Chapter three is the core of the study because it explains the guidelines and implementation considerations for a community. The chapter is divided into eight sections: waste characterization study, creation of a recycleable list and goal establishment, targeting the recycleable material, operating parameters, costs and cost effectiveness, financing the recycling program, community education, and evaluating the ongoing program. Chapter four describes one of the most important parameters of the recycling program; the marketability of recycleable materials and how to find markets.

Chapter five describes the Seattle, Washington recycling program including its history and successes. Its goals establishment, public participation, marketability of materials are standouts to the success of the program.

Chapter six culminates the study by recapitulating the highpoints of implementation, the need for federal government directive, and the future expectations for recycling.

III. Scope of the Study

The aim of this project is not to discuss the new solid waste management integrated approach in detail, but rather to focus on one element of the approach; recycling. Recycling is acquiring a growing role in the integrated approach and community acknowledgment of that fact is imperative for the future well being of the nation's communities.

The focus of the recycling element will be on how a community could implement a recycling program. The model created to display this program will be generic in nature, but at the same time specific in raising acute points of interest along with possible recommendations. The study will not attempt to create a specific implementation plan for a particular community, but rather a detailed list of points of interest. The investigator does not want to duplicate prior studies by solely describing the specific successes of model communities.

The data utilized for the project will be a mixture of

primary and secondary data. The primary data used will be from interviews with community recycling experts. The majority of the study will encompass the use of secondary data from periodicals. The purpose of the study is not to gain working knowledge of data manipulation, but to attempt to create a specific plan which may be useful to communities interested in creating and implementing a recycling program.

The conclusion of the project will probably not amaze the reader as to why communities do not spring immediately into the implementation of a recycling program. The fact is that there are often problems with recycling plans, most stemming from the lack of markets for recycleable goods and others revolving around political/budgeting constraints.

IV. Methods

The study utilizes mainly secondary data. The majority of the information was gathered from an assortment of recent periodicals dealing with specific points of interest and concern about recycling. Recently published books were used to gather information, but the majority of the information was extracted from periodicals (see bibliography).

The only primary data that was collected was from one key informant interview with a solid waste/recycling professional; Kathy Maxwell, the Solid Waste Coordinator for the City of Newport, Rhode Island. She was interviewed regarding her present day successes and struggles in implementing a recycling program within the community. Topics of discussion included the importance of evaluating "avoided costs" (chapter 3), and marketability of recycleables, and other parameters pertaining to the implementation of a community curbside recycling plan.

The document is composed of mainly narrative with a few figures and many appendices which are useful in illustrating certain points discussed within the narrative. The use of one model community (Seattle, Washington) is discussed in detail within chapter 5. Seattle is utilized to lend more validity to the community recycling concept, proving that it is indeed feasible and successful given proper planning, funding, and management.

1. Solid Waste Management: Planning Issues and Opportunities, American Planning Association (1990), 1.

2. James R. Meszaros, "Keeping Up with the Fast-Changing Rules." Solid Waste and Power, Vol. IV, No. 5 (October 1990), 46.

3. Solid Waste Management, Planning Issues and Opportunities, American Planning Association, (1990), 35.

4. Solid Waste Management: Planning Issues and Opportunities, American Planning Association (1990), 21-22.

CHAPTER TWO

CHAPTER TWO

THE RECYCLING IDEOLOGY

I. Recycling vs. Technology

Due to the increased amounts of waste produced within the nation, conventional waste management solutions with philosophies regarding resources as being infinitely vast, such as landfilling, are becoming exhausted. Past and present solutions to waste disposal are derived from engineering and technological designs and approaches. These designs are formulated in an attempt to handle the present and growing future waste stream. "The sanitary engineers have long relied on "technology" solutions and have been reluctant to become involved with production issues, consumer habits, or programs requiring high levels of public participation." [1] The recycling concept steps back from the common mechanical solution ideology, focuses on the source of the problem, and attempts to reduce and reuse materials so to minimize the inefficient use of the nation's natural resources.

The integration approach incorporates the use of incineration, recycling, landfilling and more, but sole reliance on the technological approaches is dangerous and expensive for the nation's people and environment. The incineration or "waste to energy" approach is quite expensive since it depends on costly pollution minimization devises which often require extensive maintenance. The plants can cost hundreds of million dollars and are usually constructed for only a 20 year life span. Costs for maintenance often increase as the plant becomes older and less efficient. Compounds such as dioxins and furans along with heavy metals are released into the air and their concentrations at any level have been the argument of debate in terms of their carcinogenetic role and other harmful effects such as birth defects and organ problems. [2] Even though there are a significant amount of adverse impacts and costs from the incineration process, waste management must rely on this technology for the present and future as an important element of the integration approach. It is an effective means to reduce the volume of waste in landfills by 80%. One must remember that there are negative aspects to all waste managment approaches, and there is no ideal solution.

Landfilling became prominant following World War II without much governmental regulation and were properly nicknamed "dumps". The detrimental hazards of these dumps are being exposed today as their toxic leachates are contaminating precious groundwater sources. Today, regulations have become extremely strict requiring three drainage layers, two to three natural impervious layers (clay), impervious synthetic layers, leachate collection systems, and proper landfill closure guidelines. The construction costs of the present day landfills are extraordinary. These costly landfills are usually the final resting place for "nearly 180 million tons of waste the nation annually produces". [3] This is so since this nation produces more waste per capita than any other nation in the world. [4] The need for technology is not being denied, but the sole reliance on technological solutions to the nation's waste management dilemna is too monetarily expensive and too environmentally costly. The more materials can be recycled or reused, the more waste can be extracted from the typical waste cycle. This in turn avoids costs to communities, and inevitably to the community residents/taxpayers.

The integration approach requires a certain amount of high technology, but a greater and increased reliance on simpler "common sense" solutions such as recycling are needed stemming from a change in national waste disposal philosophies. Recycling is a simple concept which is beneficial and important for the following reasons: it conserves natural resources such as trees, fuel, metals, water and land, it can cost less than landfilling or incineration, it protects our health and environment when harmful substances are removed from the waste stream, and the United States Environmental Protection Agency has set a national goal of reducing and recycling 25% of our waste by 1992. [5] Almost any municipal waste can be recycled including paper, metal, glass, and plastics.

The basis of the recycling concept incorporates four distinct phases: collection of the material, sorting by type of waste (glass, paper, etc.), reclamation (recovery of material into salvaged and usable form), and end-use (means for recovered material to be used again).[6] One of the most important aspects necessary for the effectiveness of recycling, is public awareness involving understanding, education, and enthusiasm. Without the public support, the supply side of the concept is non-existent. The supply-side of the recycling concept is the fuel that drives the system; without it, the system would be non-feasible (discussed in detail in Chapter 4).

The recycling concept is definitely not a new one even though it has only recently captured the large scale attention of the American public. In fact, organized recycling has been occuring since at least the 1920's. People have collected salvageable material for years through various means including scavenging. The practice reached an all time efficient high (35% of total waste stream) during World War II when resources were low in supply, but high in demand.[7] During the 1950's and 1960's, the recycling effort diminished with the introduction of the synthetic "one-use/throw away" products. "The United States Environmental Protection Agency estimates that Americans now generate 3.5 pounds of trash per person per day, compared with 2.7 pounds in 1960."[8] Since the introduction of the "throw away" products, the percentage of recycleables has been reduced to approximately 10% on average nationwide.[9]

Appendix A illustrates the municipal waste generation (tons) and methods of disposal by state, nationwide (1989). Methods of disposal include recycling/composting, incineration, and landfilling. According to this information, the percent recycled by state is quite small, ranging from a low of 1% to a high of 29%. Common general averages from numerous sources demonstrate that present waste disposal nationwide is handled as follows: recycling (10%), incineration (10%), and landfilling (80%).

II. "New Efficiency" Concept

American ideology has consistently focused on the "more is better" form of thought. This thought process is simply not appropriate in a time when resources are scarce and there is a growing realization that the world is not a vast and infinite dumping and extraction ground.

A recent article by W. David Stephenson entitled "'New Efficiency' Spells Change for Waste Industry" discusses how this attitude in American business will be its downfall if not altered. The essense of the "New Efficiency" philosophy and approach is "the shift from the old more-is-better attitude to an understanding that we can live better - and - profitably by doing more with less." [10] Even though the article deals directly with business and industrial waste and inefficiencies, the "New Efficiency" concept is important at the municipal level. He discusses that "less is better" is counter-intuitive because the entire American tradition has been "expansive and growth-oriented".

Stephenson stresses "cyclical and spiral thinking" rather than the traditional Western linear or hierarchical thought. [11] This thought process is the entire basis for recycling. The resources initially utilized can be saved and used again in either the same or different form, thereby creating a recycling circle. The predominant philosophy in the nation today is to extract, sell, utilize, and then dispose of the material. When one stands back, takes an unbiased view of the situation, the linear process does indeed seem extremely wasteful and inefficient.

Stephenson's "New Efficiency" promises the following benefits for the nation:

1. Less production, disposal, packaging and distribution costs because we will make products that are smaller, simpler, lighter without using as many materials to do so.
2. Less consumer and activists boycotts and regulatory, liability or disposal costs because we will learn to use wastes.
3. Less vulnerability to cartels and blockades because we will not depend as heavily on virgin resources.
4. More consumer loyalty because we will sell modular systems that are easy to upgrade.
5. More ability to compete in global markets because our products will have the clean lines and low operating costs that American consumers desire - and less-affluent consumers elsewhere demand.
6. More quality control because the products will be simpler. [12]

Overall, he states, less problems and more advantages combine for more profit in the long run.

III. The Curbside Recycling Approach

The basic definition of recycling is that it is "essentially an activity involving the transformation of a "post-consumer" material discard into a new, reformulated product." [13] There are many different approaches to recycling including "buy-back centers" (stationary or mobile) primarily for the collection of glass and metal products, apartment house carts used for multifamily dwellings, material recovery facilities (MRF's) for the magnetic separation of waste, transfer stations as midway places for municipal waste where some sorting can occur, and the "curbside recycling programs". Curbside collection programs generally cost more than other programs since collection and transportation from each individual household is involved.

The curbside collection approach is not the choice for all communities because its costs are higher than other recycling options, but it is a large and growing recycling option since it proves to provide the largest public participation rate. Some communities may not wish to utilize this approach because of reasons such as small community size (in such a case, a stationary recycling buy-back "drop-off" center may be used). The drop-off centers capture lesser amounts of recycleables, but cost less then curbside collection. Curbside recycling costs more, but captures more recycleables. Community recycling decisions must be made focusing on the desired participation rate and cost in order to determine whether to implement the curbside program or a less intensive recycling effort.

The curbside recycling process sometimes involves the initial separation of waste by individuals, but not necessarily (commingled waste), and then the curbside collection, either by the municipality itself, or by its contracted hauler, or by a private hauler who sells services independent of municipal control. The waste is then delivered to recycling centers and sold as raw materials in economic markets within a relatively close proximity. The form of the raw material is usually altered in some way by heat, pressure, or reduction to uniform particle size after the marketing of the product. Materials that are usually recycled in a typical curbside recycling program include paper, aluminum cans, steel bimetal cans (often referred to as "tin" cans), glass, and certain plastics. Although almost all municipal waste can physically be altered and reused, not all are recycled due to marketing constraints (the marketing of recyclables will be discussed in Chapter 4).

1. Solid Waste Management, Planning Issues and Opportunities, American Planning Association (1990), 5.

2. Solid Waste Management, Planning Issues and Opportunities, American Planning Association (1990), 21.

3. Solid Waste Management; Planning Issues and Opportunities, American Planning Association (1990), 1.

4. Solid Waste Managment, Planning Issues and Opportunities, American Planning Association (1990), 1.

5. "Recycle." United States Environmental Protection Agency, Office of Solid Waste, EPA/530-SW-88-050 (October 1988).

6. "The Urgent Need to Recycle," Time Magazine - The Council for Solid Waste Solutions, (July 17, 1989), 3.

7. Solid Waste Management, Planning Issues and Opportunities, American Planning Association (1990), 3.

8. James R. Meszaros, "Keeping Up with the Fast-Changing Rules." Solid Waste and Power, Vol. IV, No. 5 (October 1990), 46.

9. Solid Waste Management, Planning Issues and Opportunities, American Planning Association, 3.

10. David W. Stephenson, "New Efficiency Spells Change for Waste Industry," Waste Dynamics of New England, Vol. 1, Number 11 (February 1991), 22.

11. David W. Stephenson, "New Efficiency Spells Change for Waste Industry," Waste Dynamics of New England, Vol. 1, Number 11 (February 1991), 23.

12. David W. Stephenson, "New Efficiency Spells Change for Waste Industry," Waste Dynamics of New England, Vol. 1, Number 11 (February 1991), 23.

13. Solid Waste Management, Planning Issues and Opportunities, American Planning Association (1990), 21.

CHAPTER THREE

CHAPTER 3

COMMUNITY CURBSIDE RECYCLING GUIDELINES

I. Implementation of the Curbside Recycling Program

The previous chapter mentioned that the curbside approach is not the choice of all communities due to costs and varying community recycling goals. Many communities do proceed with the curbside approach since it has the highest participation rate of all recycling programs which stems from the convenience of home material pick-up. This chapter focuses on the implementation of a recycling program in a generic community that has intentions of proceeding with the curbside approach to maximize recycling participation and collection. The following information will be useful to communities wanting to follow in the successful footsteps of other curbside recycling programs by illustrating a semi-comprehensive description of key points of interest. Many of these guidelines and elements are in no particular order and their consideration during the planning stage may not necessarily occur in this illustrated order.

Implementing a curbside recycling program "can be described as more of an art than a science." [1] There are many factors involved with the curbside program including participation rates, public education, number of collections per week, determining the number of waste collection crews, whether to allow commingled waste or not, determination of the optimum number of collection bins, sizes of trucks, evaluation, and finding markets for recycleables. Every community differs in respect to population, street width, building type, waste stream, etcetera and relying on an exact format or model from another successful recycling community would not be effective. The one broad-based element every community must strive to acquire is a design which incorporates the best and most convenient means for the residents and the waste hauler so to achieve maximum participation and minimum costs.

II. Waste Characterization Study

The first step for a municipality is to understand is how much community waste is produced and most importantly for recycling purposes, the amounts of specific waste categories (paper, glass, metal, plastics, yard wastes). "Ultimately, effective waste stream analysis is the first step in the planning process (recycling)." [2] The following are two figures depicting the typical waste characterization percentages (averages) for municipal waste nationwide.

Figure 1, below, displays the percentage breakdown by weight, whereas Figure 2 illustrates the volume. Notice that paper is the leading fraction of the overall amount in both weight (40%) and volume (34%). Within a more affluent community, there will be an even larger percentage of newspapers. [3]

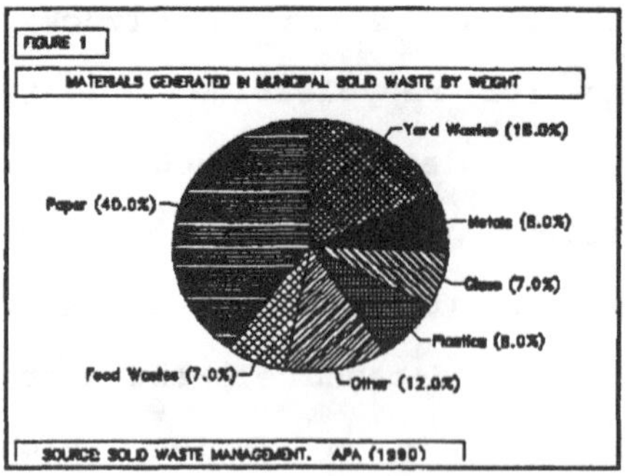

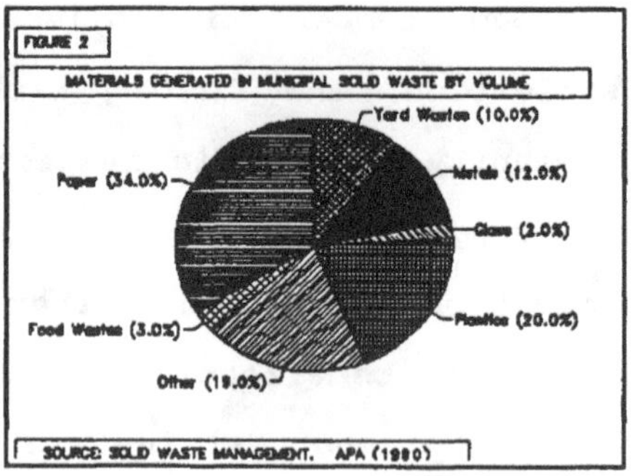

In respect to weight, yard wastes and plastics hold the second and third largest percentages respectively. Volume is what should truly be regarded since it is the volume, not the weight of the waste, that is of primary concern and impact in reaching maximum landfill capacity. Plastics and yard wastes hold second and third places respectively.

These are percentages that illustrate national figures which may or may not correspond with a sample community. A solid waste coordinator must determine the quantity of each particular waste within a specific community's waste stream. This process is commonly described as a "waste audit" or "waste characterization study". The process is not a standardized one, but does involve the sampling of waste within the waste stream in order to acquire an estimate indicative of the total waste stream. The waste audit is imperative for the planning of program design especially in relation to the marketing aspect of recycling.

III. Creation of Recycleable List and Goal Establishment

A list of recycleables which the community is considering recycling is important for the groundwork of the program. The typical list will include paper (newprint, corrugated paper, computer paper, office and other high grade paper, mixed paper), metal (aluminum cans, aluminum containers, tinned cans, bi-metal cans, ferrous metal, nonferrous metal, appliances), glass (refillable beer bottles, container glass), plastic (PET containers - polyethylene terephthalate, HDPE containers - high density polyethylene, other), and miscellaneous (vehicle batteries, tires, used oil). [4]

"Developing a list of materials for curbside collection seems simple enough. But cities dispose in landfills tons of glass collected in their recycling programs. They pay brokers or paper mills to take old newspapers off their hands. They pay ten times the collection and disposal cost to recycle plastics." [5] Situations such as this will arise more often without proper planning for marketing. The materials that do not hold promising marketing futures should remain on the list for later dates, but should not be pursued from an financial perspective. The marketing of recycleables is one of the major keys to success and therefore will be discussed in Chapter 4.

The establishment of a recycling goal is imperative for the progression of the program. The goal adds direction to the decision process focusing on the amounts of waste that should be removed from the overall waste stream. These goals are usually determined by state and local governments for two primary reasons: the Federal government has not formulated legislation mandating recycling objectives and each community differs in the amount of waste it is capable of handling. As previously mentioned, the Environmental Protection Agency has recommended a recycling goal of 25% of total waste stream by the year 1992. This has been the closest instruction the Federal government has come to creating recycling goals for states and communities.

The community's goal will determine how much of the waste stream is to be removed. Theoretically, the more waste removed, the greater the avoided disposal costs. This is not always true since the marketability of the materials plays a major role in the goal establishment. There are no typical or standard recycling goals communities strive towards. Seattle has reached a recycling goal of 24% of the waste stream in 1990 and has a long-term goal of 60% by 1998, with interim goals of 40% by 1991, and 50% by 1993.[6] This may be a high percentage to reach for many communities, but this illustrates how communities begin with an initial goal and attempt to increase the efficiency and magnitude of the program.

The importance of recycling goals is illustrated in **Appendix B** entitled, "What it Takes and What it Makes". The illustration represents the beneficial effects of goal creation and implementation on a community the size of Springfield, Illinois. The larger the recycling goal, the greater the amounts of energy (gallons) conserved from the production of more plastic bottles and the lesser the amounts of solid waste produced (weight and volume specified).

IV. Targeting the Recycleable Materials

"Some of the key decisions a manager must make in the recycling process include: which and how many materials to include, the economics of each material, and when to add the material to the program." [7] These decisions are dependent upon the present and future market for materials. Market assessments are accomplished by conducting research on each material under consideration. Contact with material brokers, handlers, and end-users can lend some insight to the waste manager as to the present and anticipated future resale values within a specified region. Transportation costs are a significant factor too.

Communities probably will not be able to market all waste items within the community because of market constraints. Those items which have a strong and steady market value and those materials with growing marketability would deserve primary consideration. The waste target list should only encompass those materials which have been determined to be cost effective in respect to collection, marketing and processing. The manager would ideally attempt to target those materials that represent the largest proportions of the waste stream so that diversion of those materials away from the costly landfill process can occur.

There is no established limit to the number of recycleables targeted for a program, but "processing systems seem to get confused once more than five or six materials are collected." [8] "Materials almost always included in curbside programs are: clear glass containers, newspapers, and tin and aluminum cans." [9] "Other materials often considered are green glass, amber glass, PET and HDPE plastic, scrap metal, used motor oil, household batteries, yard waste, corrugated cardboard, and mixed waste paper." [10] Reasons for the consideration of these materials include high visibility, developing markets, or special environmental concerns. [11]

Often times a recycling manager may implement a program slowly and increase the magnitude or scope as indicators of success occur. The detriment to this cautious approach is the increase in capital costs in the long run since machinery may need to be adjusted (re-tooled) or added to handle the collection/processing of the added wastes. The benefit of this conservative approach is the avoidance of high potential costs caused by hasty initial investments in volatile markets or unproven public participation. In respect to the timely addition of targeted recycleables to the program at a future date, "as a rule of thumb, if a curbside program has been operating for at least 12 months, participation rates are at least 70 percent, and materials are well-received by end-markets, managers can assume the residential population is ready to recycle more." [12]

V. Operating Parameters

There are numerous operating parameters for a curbside program all impact the cost of recycling. These involve all of the detailed facets of the program such as the size of the recovery facility, average number of truck stops per day, accepting commingled waste or not, the number of bins per household, most efficient truck routes, size/make of truck, the number of individuals in a collection crew, number of pickups per month, etcetera. The management and manipulation of these detailed facets of the program influences the cost of the program significantly.

All of these factors directly affect the collection and handling efficiency and impact the cost effectiveness of the program. Every community has different characteristics and therefore will require operating parameters "tailor-fit" to that particular community. Some of the recommendations made by other recycling experts based on minimizing costs and maximizing participation rates are as follows:

1. Use a private contractor for the collection of materials. "The programs that relied on a private contractor generally had a significantly higher collection efficiency (528 stops per day) than programs that utilized municipal crews (415 stops per day)."[13]

2. Single man collection crew with a large truck is usually the most cost effective. Two and three man crews have been found to add to labor costs significantly and do not contribute two to three times that of a single man. The truck should be "economically operated and maintained and yield the highest productivity (homes served or pounds collected per hour) possible." [14]

3. Recycling programs should mimic existing programs in respect to garbage collection routes, day of pickup, curbside, etcetera. [15] This promotes consistency which is beneficial to the workers and community participants.

4. Use of over-the-top, hydraulic loading truck types. [16] This type of truck allows for easy dumping of materials by the collector and increases overall collection efficiency.

5. Use of one rectangular plastic collection bin per household collecting commingled materials. The durable plastic bin is a one time cost and does not often need replacing. Separating materials is too inconvenient for the public. [17]

These are just a handful of potential operating parameter a manager must decide upon. As previously stated, each community having differing characteristics will make different decisions as to these factors. The best advice that can be given, is that they should always be aware of the implications of these seemingly small details that can significantly affect the efficiency of the program.

VI. Costs and Cost Effectiveness

The actual costs of a recycling program are high, but usually not as high as other waste management options. "The average cost of a curbside recycling program is $60 per ton in Rhode Island." [18] Just as there is no one particular model for every community, costs vary tremendously from one community to another. Indirect variables such as the operating parameters previously mentioned cause the differences in cost. The City of Newport, Rhode Island, having many extremely narrow streets and some densely populated areas, has an approximate cost of $145 per ton because of additional transportation and safety adjustments.[19] A national survey reports that new contracts between municipalities are compromising at an average recycling cost of approximately $2.00 per month per household.[20]

The costs to a community can be calculated with three broad guidelines in mind: assess costs by volume, labor is the highest expenditure, and figure in costs to prepare and deliver material to market.[21] Waste measurements should be made in relation to volume since it is the volume usually, not weight, that fills waste bins, trucks, recovery facilities, and landfills. The curbside recycling program is highly dependent on costly labor and when considering design and cost components, labor should be minimized (e.g. one man collection crews). Total expenditures incorporating variable costs such as processing, maintenance, and transportation must be estimated. The formulation of a worst case scenario might be one approach to calculating the largest potential expense occuring due to high variable costs.

Spreadsheets may be extremely useful to the waste manager

described as the amounts of money conserved by implementing a program that differs from the normal waste management strategies (landfilling and incineration). The amount of waste diverted from the landfill/incinerator is as important as the monetary return a community acquires for the material.

Even if a material does not appear to promise a high return resale value, the avoided costs caused by recycling the product can somewhat be regarded as being equivalent to high resale values. For example, newpapers do not appear to be a sensible material to recycle since they only receive $20 per ton resale value plus hauling costs, but the avoided costs of diverting them from the landfill could be significant. They are usually the largest part of a waste stream and by diverting them, the payment of tipping fees and use of expensive landfill space can be avoided.

Analysis of cost effectiveness (avoided costs) comparing curbside recycling to other waste management means such as landfilling and incineration in different proportions can occur. The comparison of the costs per unit for each method of disposal, displaying tipping fees for landfilling, will usually indicate to the politician that recycling is more cost effective. Diminishing landfill capacity and the extremely high costs of sitin new landfills, the political difficulty of siting new landfills, all contribute significantly to a local political decision to choose recycling.

Appendix D illustrates the average landfill and

incinerator disposal costs and remaining landfill capacity (years) by state, nationwide, as of 1989. Costs for landfilling and incineration apparently vary quite significantly from state to state. Numbers such as these can be produced and compared to recycling costs by the municipality to display the avoided costs incurred by recycling. The gap (avoided costs) between the costs of implementing a recycling program and actual costs of landfilling and incineration are expected to increase significantly as landfill space for municipal solid waste and incinerator ash decreases.

One innovative means for measuring cost effectiveness has been termed "Life Cycle Costing" and involves the sum of all costs associated with a particular product from the initial production to the final disposal. [23] This process tends to increase differences of costs between recycling and alternate disposal strategies. The cost effectiveness and avoided cost approach is the key to convincing politicians that recycling is important, but the other prominent aspect of the recycling is that it stresses conservation which brings numerous qualitative benefits to society including cleaner air, land, and water. Life Cycle costing attempts to quantify the costs to society involved in the pollution and human health effects of mining, manufacture, and distribution of products before they are sold, used, and disposed of. For example, while the cost of recycled paper is high, the life cycle cost of trees and carbon dioxide hydrocarbons caused by transport is higher than the costs of using recycled paper. The main difference between the conventional cost effective analysis and life cycle costing is that life cycle costing broadens the scope of analysis to involve societal costs such as public health, safety, and welfare.

VII. Financing the Recycling Program

The program can be financed, theoretically, in different ways. Some theorists claim that by using the existing capital costs of the existing waste management strategy (which is already financed), with proper planning and management and with an average resale value for recycleables of $60 or better per ton, the curbside program would be self-financed. [24] The key to the success of this theory is that resale monies are high enough to cover all additional capital and variable costs (especially transportation). The most common means for funding a curbside program is through the use of taxes or grants.

Recent experts are noticing that most recycling programs are not self-financed and need some sort of additional funding. As previously mentioned, only approximately 22% of the program costs are recovered though the resale of materials. Recycling municipalities utilize regular municipal waste collection work crews/trucks plus recycling collection work crews and trucks. They are not able finance both municipal waste and recycling handling easily without additional funding (especially during the recycling start-up period).

Initial recycling costs will often be covered by municipal general funds, but this presents a problem in the future if the general funds are not available. [25] The recycling manager needs to receive consistent funding for the annual expenses. Often, managers can rely on the state government to allocate a certain amount of funds for municipal recycling.

The states often mandate communities reaching recycling goals within a specified amount of time. Funds are allocated annually for the implementation of the program, but often the funds only last a few years. This predicament again forces municipalities to seek alternative and reliable funding sources. One alternate means for securing an annual funding source is fees or taxes. [26]

Taxing is a always a sensitive issue for the public, therefore, consideration to "how much money is needed and when; who should bear the burden of the program costs; how complex is the tax, and whether a particular funding mechanism has appropriate funding incentives to minimize waste." [27] Every aspect of the tax and what its goals are must be well established. The following are some potential taxes or surcharges that could be considered for gaining revenue:

1. "Waste-end" (tipping fee) taxes; Imposed on final waste acceptors (landfills and incinerators), which will pass this cost onto the residents. One problem with this is that there is an incentive to recycle, and as recycling levels increase, waste disposal decreases, leaving less waste to tax and less revenue. These charges often range from $.25 - 19.00 per ton. [28]

2. "Disposal Fees"; Imposed on purchasers of particular waste items that pose a significant problem with disposal (e.g. tires, batteries, anti-freeze). The tax range is usually between $.25 - 2.00 per item. [29]

3. "Product-Based Disposal" taxes; Imposed on manufactures based on the materials used in the products and packaging. Ideally, charges would reflect the cost of disposal. The tax must be high enough to induce conservation, but not too high to deter manufacturers from residing in the area. [30]

4. "Litter" taxes; Imposed on businesses on either all or simply the ones determined to be litter producing (e.g. beer and wine). It is recommended that all be taxed and reduce the tax rate, thereby, no particular businesses would be incriminated. [31]

5. "Deposit Programs" (Bottle Bills); Imposed on consumers for the purchase of certain containers (e.g. beverage). These programs are incentive producers for people to return containers, but money is usually made since people do not always return the containers to acquire their monetary returns. [32]

6. "Credit Systems and Processing Fees"; Imposed on manufacturers in which they must guarantee some minimum level of recycling or minimum value for their product. With the credit approach, "manufacturers can fulfill this guarantee by recycling the products themselves or purchasing a recycling credit from an independent recycler (pay someone else to handle recycling)." "The processing-fee has two options: the manufacturers can guarantee scrap prices sufficient to cover the costs of recycling; or they may pay the government a processing fee equal to the difference for each product sold." Also, if market prices fall, the

> manufacturers must pay the difference to the government. It is a radical approach, but does directly involve businesses in the recycling market. Revenue is acquire, theoretically, during times of economic downturn.[33]

In almost all cases nationwide, avoided costs provide base financing. The above options are potential additional sources. Fees to manufacturers and distributors are a consistently tremendous political difficulty. Special taxes and fees require expensive enforcement and administrative mechanisms resulting in less money for actual operations. Federal action may be needed in the future to assess fair fees on manufacturers.

VIII. Community Education

Community education is one of the most important aspects of a program since it leads to public acceptance and recycling success. Public education about the community recycling program should occur before and during the curbside program so to inform/reinforce the benefits of recycling and also to notify individuals of any alterations or additions to the recycling program (e.g. addition of new targeted collectables). Whether a program is voluntary or mandatory, public willingness to accept a recycling program will promote overall success.

There are various means for building the exposure of a curbside recycling program. School systems can educate people at a younger age through the use of distributed literature

and/or volunteer spokespeople. "The school system approach is based on the concept that if you educate the child, you educate the adult." [34] Another route to public education is through direct mailings and newsletters by the United States Post Office, utility companies, and other businesses. The recycling program in Cincinnati, Ohio publisized its program by attaching brochures to the recycling bins as they were distributed. [35] The acquistion of media support (television, radio, newspaper, cable) is also another significantly efficient avenue for informing the public. The costs of stimulating and increasing public education have been estimated by a national poll to range from
$.10 - 4.00. [36]

The Ocean State Cleanup and Recycling Program (OSCAR) a division of D.E.M. of Rhode Island recommends a personal incentive approach to public education. "High participation rates and outstanding individual efforts should be recognized and rewarded. The money saved through recycling efforts might be used for charity donations, social activities or individual awards." [37] OSCAR also states the importance of feedback. The progress of the program should be communicated to the community by mentioning for example "how much revenue is earned and how much is saved through avoided disposal costs." [38]

The best means for acquiring ongoing public education and maintaining the link between the program managers and participants is a telephone recycling hotline. The hotline provides those individuals with questions or difficulties assistance with the program. The hotline can provide individual information on the recycleables accepted, when pickup occurs in their location, how recycleables should be handled, and other comprehensive information about the curbside program.

IX. Evaluating the Ongoing Program

Every program differs in form and structure, and there are no standardized means for evaluation. Cost comparisons with other conventional disposal methods are not always the best means for judging a program. "For example, comparisons with landfill expenditures are not always appropriate. Cincinnati embarked upon its recycling program without experiencing a waste disposal crisis or having incurred excessive landfill costs." [39] This costs the city more than the conventional landfill method, but the city regards this as an investment in its future. [40]

Even though there are no "hard and fast" rules in respect to evaluating ongoing curbside recycling programs, there are two measurements often used: participation rates and set-out rates.

These can be used to examine past to present trends in the recycling program.

"Set-out rates refer to the number of residences actually setting out bins over a period of time, usually a month." [41]

These can be directly influenced by the demographic trends of the community. If there are numerous elderly, the rate will not be so high, whereas, if there are many children, the rate will be higher since the waste stream will differ.

"Participation rates refer to the number of households participating in the program, by not routinely setting out recycleables." [42] This number can differ from the set-out rate if residences save their materials for periods longer than one week within their homes, but this does not mean they are not participating in the program. The National Recycling Council has adopted a formula to translate set-out rates into participation rates: participation rates are generally twice the set-out rates. [43] More specific participation rates can be acquired by taking periodic samplings of the residents over time. This can be accomplished by manual or electronic sampling. St. Louis Park, Minnesota uses bar codes attached to each container which count each bin filled as an indicator of participation. [44] As a point of reference, the average participation rate nationwide is approximately 75 percent.[45]

The measure of percent of waste recycled can also be utilized in comparison to realistic recycling goals as another indicator. Unrealistic goals should not be utilized for forms of comparison since this will only display unsatisfactory evidence. These are often termed "before and after" studies.

The evaluation of the community's recycling vendor is also important so to determine the depth of commitment, since they can directly influence whether or not a community succeeds or fails. A vendor that can assist with initial start-up costs having good credit and reputation is imperative. The ability of the vendor to find end-markets should also be considered. The manager should also expect the vendor to lend some expertise and consideration in the form of marketing, community recycling education, and flexibility.

1. Jim Glenn, "Curbside Recycling Reaches 40 Million." Biocycle, (July 1990), 31.

2. Solid Waste Management, Planning Issues and Opportunities, American Planning Association (1990), 13.

3. Kathy Maxwell. Interview (April 1991).

4. Gene E. Patterson "How Much Does Recycling Reduce the Waste Stream." Biocycle (July 1990), 49.

5. Susan J. Smith and Leslie C. Shera, "Material Selection: Avoiding the Pitfalls." Solid Waste and Power, Vol. V, Number 1 (February 1991), 36.

6. Rodd Zolkos, "Seattle Not so Green to Innovative Recycling." City and State, (October 8, 1990), R4.

7. Susan J. Smith and Leslie C. Shera, "Material Selection: Avoiding the Pitfalls." Solid Waste and Power, (October 1991), 36.

8. Susan J. Smith and Leslie C. Shera, "Material Selection: Avoiding the Pitfalls." Solid Waste and Power, Vol. V, Number 1, (February 1991), 38.

9. Smith and Shera, 38.

10. Smith and Shera, 38.

11. Smith and Shera, 38.

12. Smith and Shera, 40.

13. Glenn, 36.

14. How To Implement A Plastics Recycling Program, Council for Solid Waste Solutions (1991), 37.

15. How to Implement A Plastics Recycling Program, 32.

16. How To Implement A Plastics Recycling Plastics Program, 32.

17. How To Implement A Plastics Recycling Program, 32.

18. Kathy Maxwell, Interview (April 1991).

19. Kathy Maxwell, Interview (April 1991).

20. Jim Glenn, "Curbside Recycling Reaches 40 Million", Biocycle, (July 1990), 37.

1. How to Implement a Plastics Recycling Program, 45.

2. Glenn, 37.

3. Kathy Maxwell, Interview (April 1991).

4. Barbara J. Stevens, "How To Finance Curbside Recycling." Biocycle (February 1989), 31.

5. Carol Andress, "Options for Funding Recycling Programs." Solid Waste and Power, (December 1990), 48.

6. Andress, 48.

7. Andress, 48.

8. Andress, 50.

9. Andress, 50

10. Andress, 50.

11. Andress, 50.

12. Andress, 50.

13. Andress, 53.

14. Glenn, 37.

15. James R. Meszaros, "Keeping up with the Fast Changing Rules." Solid Waste and Power. Vol. IV, Number 5, (October 1990), 48.

16. Glenn, 37.

17. Rhode Island Department of Environmental Protection. Guide for Preparing Solid Waste Reduction and Recycling Plans for Multi-Family Residential Units. 6.

18. Rhode Island DEM, 6.

19. Meszaros, 50.

20. Meszaros, 50.

21. Meszaros, 50

22. Meszaros, 50.

23. Meszaros, 52.

44. Glenn, 31.

45. Glenn, 31.

CHAPTER FOUR

CHAPTER 4

MARKETING OF THE RECYCLEABLES

I. Basis for Marketing in Recycling

Marketing is the driving force behind recycling. Without an end-buyer for the materials, there will be a surplus of collected materials that ultimately end up in the same process recycling attempts to avoid; landfilling. The following analogy describes the market system of recycling. "The flow of materials is similar to the flow of water in a plumbing system. If the flow in the pipeline is too fast, the plumbing system becomes backed up; if the flow is too slow, the trickle may not be sufficient to operate the system." [1]

"Success in recycling is not measured by intensity, desire or concern for the environment we live in, but rather by careful planning and consistent implementation of programs that capitalize on the economic conditions that surround recycling as an industry." [2] The recycling loop is closed only when recycled materials are sold and reused. This recycling loop is not always closed at present especially as with certain paper and plastic materials. Processing is not able to handle the overabundant supply.

II. Understanding the Recycleable Market

There are three specific questions that must be answered regarding the understanding of a specific market for recycleables, and they are as follows: who needs or wants the product?, why do they need or want it?, and how do they choose one version of the product over a competing version? [3] The answers to these can be found by consulting marketing experts or teams. Often, personnel from the materials recovery facility, through which the contract is held, will be allocated the responsibility of understanding all facets of the particular market.

The buyers of the materials include dealers/processors, wholesalers, brokers, and others. The manufacturers are ones who create the demand for a particular recycleable. "It is that demand which "pulls" materials through the distribution channels." [4]

These manufacturers directly influence the amounts paid for the products by various means. First, supply and demand; the more they demand a product (which is often determined by consumer habits), the more they will be willing to pay, but the more of an oversupply there is, the less the product is worth. Second, "minimum production capacity" of the buying industry influences the market value. Even if there is a demand for a product, if processing of materials can not reach an equilibrium with supply, the value of that recycleable will decrease (e.g. newspaper). Third, "limits on substitutability" can detrimentally affect product quality. Mixed plastics, metals, and paper often produce inferior grades of each material and may be cheaper for the manufacturer to simply utilize virgin resources than attempting to retrofit secondary product manufacturing. Fourth, the plentiful "availability of virgin feedstocks" often forces the value downward which also affects the resale values of that particular material as a recycleable. [5]

III. Finding Markets for the Community Recycleables

Most would recommend finding markets before the community collection stage since a recycling manager does not want to be left with a surplus of materials. Although this appears to be the most practical and conservative approach, there is at least one successful individual that recommends community stimulation of a market. Joan Edwards, the director of integrated solid waste management for the City of Los Angeles, California recommends "a concurrent method of developing markets for recycleables at the same time that you begin to collect the materials." [6] She states that this has often times forced market development within the area because entrepreneurs will often realize an oversupply of a material and will develop a market for it. This is feasible only if there is storage capacity for collected recycleables in the case that a portion are not immediately sold.

Overseas markets are available especially to those on the west coast. The reliability of these markets is not always as stable as within the nation principally due to varying shipping capacity at ports. Also, many would rather sell to national markets so to give opportunity to American businesses.

As previously stated, most recommend having the security of a pre-existing market before the collection and handling occurs. Joan Edwards recommends the practice of networking to locate markets. Another method is to rely on national agencies to lend expertise as to which markets exist and where. One agency that provide this assistance is The Council for Solid Waste Solutions which has a database of more than 700 companies that deal with recycleable materials.

Conducting a market survey is useful to the recycling manager since it will produce a potential list of handlers and also allows the manager to compare so to find the most economical and efficient market. [7] While conducting the survey, the manager should ask questions such as the following to fully understand the parameters of each potential market: 8

1. How does the market want to receive material?
2. Who will separate the materials?
3. Does the market want the material loose, baled, compacted, or bagged?
4. Can caps, labels, and rings be left on?
5. What percentage of collected unacceptable material is allowed?
6. What materials are unacceptable even in small quantities?
7. Will the market pick up the material or does it have to be delivered?

8. Are minimum quantities of material required?

9. Will the market provide services, such as equipment leases, promotional materials, technical assistance?

10. How much will the market pay for the material?

This is just a sample of questions that be included in the survey.

Some experts recommend the use of mandatory recycling for a community. Since the mandatory recycling will promote a consistent supply of high quality material, often times markets will find the community.[9] This has recently occurred in the City of Philadelphia, Pennsylvania. It seems apparent that businesspeople are willing to offer a market to communities as long as material supply can be consistantly provided.

Once a market has been found and the bidding process completed, the high quality and consistency of the materials can help a community be competitive, sell recycleables, and continue to find other markets. Each purchaser has a established set of criteria for the recycleable material in respect to what size and volume they should be presented for sale; other specifications include length of commitment, price, and transportation. [10] If these specifications are met, the community is in no jeopardy of being left with a rejected material load, thereby, maintaining a good relationship with the market that exists.

IV. Stimulating Secondary Material Markets

Many recycling experts claim that there needs to be a national market stimulation impetus since it is the federal government that has the power to lend incentive and alter the cost effectiveness for secondary material markets. Private industry has taken steps to improve markets for recycleables. Presently, there are more de-inking paper plants and plastic recycling plants planned to come on line within one to two years. Although private industry is taking some initiative, Federal backing is still seen as being imperative to the success of a nationwide recycling campaign so that markets can catch up to the oversupply of materials.

Appendix E illustrates the present market values for materials by region, nationwide. The materials that appear to have the lowest resale values per ton include newspaper and mixed waste paper. The resale of mixed waste paper in the Northeast and South is so low that additional monies are paid to brokers to accept the material. Situations similar to this simulate market failure which acually costs municipalities more than to simply initially landfill the product. Strong markets are indicated for aluminum and plastic.

Recycling experts attribute these lower resale values to the lack of governmental tax incentives given to the use of secondary materials. Also, incentives are presently given by the Federal Government to continue the extraction of virgin materials. Experts suggest that consumer habits and desires are changing to a more conservative and environmentally conscious behavior. "There was a 40 percent increase in customers using cloth diaper services between 1988 and 1989 as an alternative to disposable diapers." [11] With consumer trends changing and impacting market demand, it seems as though the Federal government will soon alter the direction of its tax incentives so to allow industry to begin the extremely expensive process of retrofitting its machinery to more efficiently handle the processing of secondary materials. Many claim that it is only consumer demands (purchasing only recycleable and recycled materials) that will alter the material processing situation and force government and industry to cater to their desires. Powerfull lobbies, especially in the paper industry, will fight to keep there preferential treatment regarding virgin materials.

How To Implement A Plastics Recycling Program, The Council for Solid Waste Solutions, 11.

__________, "Forecasting 1991." *New England Waste Resources*, (January 1991), 6.

Anton J. Finelli, "Secondary Materials Markets: A Primer." *Solid Waste and Power* (August 1990), 48.

Finelli, 50.

Finelli, 52.

Kimberly Hedzik. "Networking, Education, and Common Sense." *Waste Age* (August 1990), 68.

How To Implement A Plastics Recycling Program, Council for Solid Waste Solutions, 19.

How To Implement A Plastics Recycling Program, The Council for Solid Waste Solutions, 20.

Nancy J. Weissman. "Finding and Developing Recycling Markets." *Solid Waste and Power*, June 1990, 32.

Finelli, 56.

Richard M. Kashmanian, Trisha Ferrand, Andrew Stoeckle, and Tapio L Kuusinen. "Source Reduction and Recycleability: Recent Marketplace Activities." *Resource Recycling* (July 1990), 87.

CHAPTER FIVE

CHAPTER FIVE

RECYCLING WITHIN THE CITY OF SEATTLE, WASHINGTON

I. Seattle Recycling Program

The curbside recycling program in Seattle, Washington has received much publicity and notoriety for its successes. Although the model can not be duplicated, its success should be praised and used as a focal point to inspire other communities to also formulate successful programs.

The Seattle program received the City and State Recycling Achievement Award for 1990, and a $100,000 grant from the Ford Foundation and the John F. Kennedy School of Government at Harvard University as one of 10 winners of the 1990 Innovations in State and Local Government Awards. The program has also received awards from the Institute for Local Self-Reliance, the National Recycling Coalition, the Washington State Department of Ecology, and Recycle America. The curbside recycling program serves 79,000 households in the southern section of Seattle and 69,000 households in the northern section. The program does not include 84,000 households in buildings of five units or more. Overall, there are 253,925 tons per year of municipal waste in the Seattle waste stream and the recycling program collects 17,787 tons (South) and 22,925 tons (North) of this waste per year. The materials collected include: newpaper, mixed paper, bimetal cans, aluminum, glass, and PET plastic. The northern section separates its materials into three bins, whereas, the southern section is allowed to commingle its materials. The pick-up schedule is weekly for the North and monthly for the South. Collection is provided for the North by Waste Management/Recycle America and for the South by Rabanco/Recycle Seattle. Processing is done by two plants, each in the collections areas. The annual program cost is $1,134,121 for the North and $964,098 for the South. These costs are funded by Seattle's trash collection fees. The average disposal cost per ton is approximately $132.00 which includes $82.00 for administrative and collection costs. [1]

The North is collected by Waste Management/Recycle America and receives approximately $50.00 per ton adjusted by the Consumer Price Index. The collector also is allowed to keep the resale amount of all the materials on condition that the company also accepts all the risks involved in marketing the materials, such as having to sell at lower market rates. [2]

The South is collected by Rabanco/Recycle Seattle and also receives $50.00 per ton. This contract differs in that the city shares a profit/risk arrangement. [3]

II. Brief History of Seattle's Solid Waste Dilemna

Seattle has a population of 470,000 and presently handles its waste through an intensive, voluntary (incentive based) curbside recycling program. The program was developed because of serious problems encountered in the early 1980's.

The City's solid waste managment was handled by the Seattle Solid Waste Utility. Their duties involved collection contracts, transfer stations, and long-haul transfer to city-owned and operated landfills. [4] The two landfills were leaking and were listed as Environmental Protection Agency Superfund sites. Costs for cleanup and closing were estimated at $90 million. [5] When Seattle was forced to haul waste to a nearby King County landfill, disposal costs skyrocketed from $11.00 to $31.50 per ton. [6] Initially, Seattle investigated the incineration option, but was concerned with the environmental effects. Finally, the city seriously considered the "maximum recycling" option.

III. Planning for the Implementation

The first step the city undertook, after making the decision to recycle, and to fund this program with the monies it avoided spending on incineration, was to conduct a waste stream composition analysis. The Solid Waste Utility analyzed 580 samples from four types of waste streams over a 12 month period in 1988 and 1989. The four types are as follows: [7]

1. Residential waste picked up weekly by city-contracted haulers;
2. Waste that was hauled by residents into the two city-owned transfer stations;
3. Commercial waste hauled to private transfer stations by the two franchised waste haulers; and

4. "Pure loads" of waste, which are gathered by trucks hauling the waste of specific types of businesses.

The second step was to build a "Recycling Potential Assessment Model." [8] The forecast served three functions: it forecasts waste stream growth and private recycling over a 20 year period; analyzes the impact of waste reduction and recycling programs on materials in the waste stream; and is used to develop long term system rates and anticipate costs. [9] The components of the "Recycling Potential Assessment Model" are as follows: [10]

1. Analyze waste stream generation - sites and sources; forecasting present and future waste generation;

2. Programatic recycling - calculates program tonnage and costs by using data from waste stream generation;

3. System cost and revenue requirements - calculates the costs effects of recycling programs on the total cost of the solid waste management system.

"The results of these analyses found that the scenarios with the highest levels of recycling did not cost more and, in most cases, cost less than scenarios with lower recycling rates. The model also displayed that as disposal costs rose, there would be an increase in recycling and less demand for disposal." [11]

IV. Recycling Success in Seattle

Today, Seattle has a 75% community participation rate

(highest in the nation) and recycles approximately 30% of the total waste stream with a 50% goal by 1993, and 60% by 1998. [12] It has increased its targeted materials to also include disposable diapers, latex paint, and household hazardous wastes. "The old latex paint is collected and the light colors are mixed to form "Seattle beige," which is sold for $5.00 a gallon." [13]

One of the major attributable keys to success was the public enthusiasm which was created through a joint city-contractor education program. [14] The public awareness element included public service announcements, direct mail, booths in shopping malls, participation in community events, door-to-door work, brochures printed on recycled paper, and a block leader program called "Friends of Recycling". [15] Telephone lines had to be installed with a customer service staff and a 24-hour Message Hot Line due to the overwhelming public interest. Stemming from this is public understanding and enthusiasm towards the recycling program which translates into higher participation rates and a more cost-efficient program. There was $5 million allocated to the program in 1990, and $700,000 of that was devoted to promotion and public information programs to maintain this public interest and dedication. [16]

The program also has a regular waste variable disposal rate. The more household disposes of waste, the more expensive the rate is. This creates an incentive to recycle as much as possible. Disposal costs for the 19-gallon mini-can is $10.70, 32-gallon can is $13.75, 60-gallon is $22.75, and 90-gallon is $31.75 per month. [17] Prior to the mini-can variable rate plan, households averaged 3.5 cans (32-gallon size) per week. Today, the average residential use is 1.4 cans, and 86 percent of the community uses one container or less. [18] There are approximately 1,110 households that have even managed to generate no waste, but they must still pay a $5.95 monthly charge. [19]

The marketability of the materials is fairly strong, although there are recent reported signs of decreasing market values for newspaper and mixed paper. Although domestic markets are not strong, the city is still able to sell newspaper and mixed paper at lower value overseas in Asia.

Presently, the program has been evaluated as being marginally cost-effective. Estimates of savings (avoided costs) are between $1.00 to $5.00 per ton. [20] Even if the program broke even at this point in time, it is worth the investment because of the savings in capital costs and the landfill disposal costs are likely to increase substantially in the next few years. This increase in landfill costs will only widen the avoided cost margin between recycling and traditional waste management approaches.

Mary-Jane Kamberg. "Recycling Cuts Disposal Costs in Seattle." Solid Waste and Power (August 1990), 62.

Kamberg, 61.

Kamberg, 61.

Solid Waste Management: Planning Issues and Opportunities, American Planning Association, 52.

Solid Waste Management: Planning Issues and Opportunities, 52.

Solid Waste Management: Planning Issues and Opportunities, 52.

Solid Waste Management: Planning Issues and Opportunities, 52.

Solid Waste Management; Planning Issues and Opportunities, 52.

Solid Waste Management: Planning Issues and Opportunities, 52.

Solid Waste Management: Planning Issues and Opportunities, 53.

Solid Waste Management: Planning Issues and Opportunities, 54.

Kamberg, 61.

Rodd Zolkos. "Seattle Not So Green To Innovative Recycling." City and State (October 8, 1990), R4.

Kamberg, 63.

Kamberg, 63.

Rodd Zolkos. "Seattle Not So Green To Innovative Recycling." City and State (October 8, 1990), R4.

Kamberg, 63.

Kamberg, 64.

Zolkos, R4.

Kamberg, 65.

CHAPTER SIX

CHAPTER SIX

CONCLUSION

I. Need for Federal Involvement

The fact that Americans are the largest producers of waste in the world appears to signal that the problem of waste management is not a lack of sufficient high technological "band-aid" solutions, but a lack of conservation in regard to the nation's resources (air, water, land). As long as peoples' waste appears to be be so easily disposable, they will continue to dispose vast quantities readily. Public education and awareness must be instituted so that waste can be reduced at the source and problems in the near and far future can be minimized. As landfill space diminishes and the number of new landfills receiving permits diminishes, disposal costs will inevitably rise significantly. This lack of capacity will eventually widen the gap between landfilling/incineration and recycling in relation to cost effectiveness.

There have been numerous national surveys that illustrate a national popular desire to recycle. The recycling markets within certain parts of the country (e.g. Northeast) need boosts from government. Federal government could assist these recycling markets by diverting the tax incentives from the promotion of virgin material extraction to the promotion of the utilization of secondary materials. Government could also assist in mandating the use of recycleable paper in all governmental offices. The State of Connecticut in 1990 enacted legislation requiring a gradually increasing percentage of recycled fiber content in all newspapers sold within the state. This has stimulated the paper industry to plan to open several new recycled paper mills in the Northeast over the next five years. Numerous industries (e.g. paper) need funding to retrofit existing machinery so that they can shift towards a system utilizing more secondary materials.

II. Study Recapitulation

This study illustrated the generic but specific guidelines and points of concern for recycling; specifically those pertaining to the implementation of a community curbside recycling program. Key guidelines included waste characterization studies, creation of recycleable list and goal establishment, establishing favorable marketing contracts within reasonable hauling distance, operating parameters, costs and cost effectiveness, financing the program, the importance of community education, and the evaluation of the ongoing program.

The marketability of the recycleables is one of the most important facets of a program since it determines whether the material completed the "recycling loop" or if it will reside back in the landfill/incinerator process. The marketing facet of recycling should be considered as part of the implementation guidelines.

The Seattle, Washington model was described in some detail and appeared to correspond for the most part to the guidelines illustrated in chapter three (guidelines for plan). The City's dedication and innovation should be recognized, as it has, and other communities should strive to also devise programs just as successful as that model.

The main focus of this study was recycling, and high technological approaches to the solid waste situation were often downplayed as being only short-term solutions and approaches that lend incentive to produce more waste. This author would like to express that the use of high technological solutions, such as waste to energy incineration, are indeed realized as necessary. Recycling can not at this present time capture the total waste stream, and it is questionable as to whether it ever will. The <u>sole</u> use of these high technological approaches without conservation practices is what is difficult to accept.

The integrated approach involving the Environmental Protection Agency's hierarchical order of waste reduction, recycling, composting, incineration, and landfilling is a system which would accomplish efficient, conservative, and total waste management. At present, there are missing pieces in that hierarchy which makes the system inefficient from a holistic perspective. Recycling and alternative conservative means for municipal solid waste management must begin to be more introduced into this hierarchy.

The future of recycling displays mixed indicators. Public acceptance and anticipation are high, but markets need stimulation. Due to market and economic constraints, recycling is expected to face some adversity through the 1990's. As previously mentioned, consumer trends/demand may be the one major factor that will influence government and industry to accomodating secondary markets, thereby, creating a demand for secondary materials. Soaring landfill and incineration costs will also affect more consumers as time goes on. As consumers are affected by disposal prices, their preference for both recycling and purchasing recycling products will grow. Currently, there are efforts by government, mostly state and county, to discourage overpackaging, environmentally irresponsible packaging, and non-recycleable packaging. This effort combined with consumer habits will definitely influence the recycling market in the future.

APPENDIX A

WASTE GENERATION AND METHODS OF DISPOSAL (BY STATE), 1989

State	Population	MSW Generation (in tons)	Percent Recycled/ Composted	Percent Incinerated	Percent Landfilled
Alabama	4,100,000	4,400,000	5%	2%	93%
Alaska	500,000	450,000	5	8	87
Arizona	3,400,000	3,100,000	Unk	0	100
Arkansas	2,400,000	1,800,000a	5	3	92
California	27,700,000	44,000,000b	12	2	86
Colorado	3,300,000	2,000,000	14	0	86
Connecticut	3,300,000	2,900,000	Unk	63	37
Delaware	650,000	600,000	4/16	43	37
Dist. of Columbia	600,000	740,000	5	20	75
Florida	12,000,000	16,000,000c	4/1	21	75
Georgia	6,200,000	4,400,000	Unk	5	95
Hawaii	1,100,000	1,000,000	4	13	83
Idaho	1,000,000	750,000	3	2	95
Illinois	11,600,000	15,000,000	6	2	92
Indiana	5,500,000	3,500,000	5	10	85
Iowa	2,800,000	2,300,000a	7-10	2	88-91
Kansas	2,500,000	1,600,000	5	0	95
Kentucky	3,700,000	4,600,000a	Unk	0	100
Louisiana	3,500,000	3,500,000d	2	0	98
Maine	1,200,000	900,000	6	57	37
Maryland	4,500,000	7,200,000	Unk	25	75
Massachusetts	5,900,000	6,600,000	7	48	45
Michigan	9,200,000	11,700,000	Unk	4	96
Minnesota	4,200,000	4,000,000	15/1	18	66
Mississippi	2,600,000	1,800,000	Unk	4	96
Missouri	5,100,000	5,100,000a	7	1	92
Montana	800,000	600,000	Unk	4	96
Nebraska	1,500,000	1,100,000	8-10	0	90-92
Nevada	1,000,000	1,000,000	5	0	95
New Hampshire	1,100,000	1,000,000e	5	33	62
New Jersey	7,600,000	9,500,000	18	2	80
New Mexico	1,500,000	1,000,000	1	0	99
New York	17,800,000	20,000,000	10	13	77
North Carolina	6,400,000	6,000,000a	Unk	1	99
North Dakota	650,000	450,000	1	0	99
Ohio	10,800,000	13,900,000a	5	10	85
Oklahoma	3,300,000	2,700,000	2	17	81
Oregon	2,700,000	2,200,000c	22	9	69
Pennsylvania	12,000,000	9,200,000	2	3	95
Rhode Island	1,000,000	1,000,000	13	0	87
South Carolina	3,400,000	3,900,000	8	2	90
South Dakota	700,000	750,000	1	0	99
Tennessee	4,800,000	3,900,000a	Unk	13	87
Texas	16,800,000	17,800,000e	8	1	91
Utah	1,700,000	1,100,000	Unk	12	88
Vermont	550,000	330,000d	12	10	78
Virginia	5,900,000	9,000,000e	8-12	10	78-82
Washington	4,500,000	5,200,000	29/1	1	70
West Virginia	1,900,000	2,500,000	Unk	0	100
Wisconsin	4,800,000	3,600,000a	Unk/1	13	87
Wyoming	500,000	550,000	5	0	95
TOTALS	245,650,000	268,220,000			

Unk: Figure is unknown.
a. Includes some industrial waste.
b. Includes some sewage sludge and demolition waste.
c. Includes demolition waste.
d. Includes some sewage sludge.
e. Includes some demolition and industrial waste.

JRCE: *Solid Waste Management, Issues and Opportunities*, American Planning Association (1990), 14.

APPENDIX B

WHAT IT TAKES AND WHAT IT MAKES

This chart illustrates how recycling can reduce the energy used in manufacturing and the wastes created in disposing of 1 year's worth of PET soft drink bottles used by a town the size of Springfield, Illinois.*

	TAKES	MAKES	
Recycling rate	**Energy used** (in gallons of gasoline)	**Solid waste produced** Weight	Volume
0%	174,400 gallons	528,493 lbs.	32,033 cubic feet
At current 20% recycling rate	164,000 gallons	461,831 lbs.	26,450 cubic feet
50%	147,200 gallons	361,839 lbs.	18,128 cubic feet
75%	133,600 gallons	278,512 lbs.	11,124 cubic feet

*Population figures based on 1980 census

SOURCE: *Solid Waste Management, Issues and Opportunities*, American Planning Association (1990), 24.

APPENDIX C

Total Annual Recycling System Costs

Use this section to tabulate the annual cost of collection, processing and transportation to market using worksheets A through F on the following pages. For example, to determine the cost to be included on line (A), complete worksheet (A) and carry the total to the appropriate line.

The annual cost of collection	$________	(A)
Plus the cost of processing	+$________	(B)
Plus the cost of transportation to market	+$________	(C)
Minus the total revenues received from the sale of each recyclable material	−$________	(D)
Minus the savings from reduced refuse collection costs (based on the volume diverted from the refuse collection route)	−$________	(E)
Minus the savings from reduced refuse tipping fees (based on the volume saved if landfilling, tonnage if incinerating)	−$________	(F)
Equals the net annual cost/savings of recycling	=$________	

JRCE: How To Implement A Plastics Recycling Program, The Council for Solid Waste Solutions, 46-55.

APPENDIX C

(A) To Determine the Annual Collection Costs:

Operating Costs

1. Labor (wages, taxes, benefits)[1] $__________
2. Plus all vehicle operating/maintenance costs[2] +$__________
3. Plus other collection/storage equipment (e.g., drop boxes) maintenance costs +$__________
4. Plus education/promotion costs +$__________
5. Plus overhead and other operating costs[3] +$__________

Equals total operating costs =$__________

Capital Costs (amortized)

6. Collection trucks $__________
7. Plus specialized equipment[4] +$__________
8. Plus household set-out bins or bags[5] +$__________
9. Plus storage containers (e.g., drop boxes) +$__________
10. Plus other capital costs +$__________

Equals total capital costs (amortized) =$__________

Total annual collection costs
(sum of operating and capital costs) =$__________(A)

(B) To Determine the Annual Processing Costs:

Operating Costs

11. Labor (wages, taxes, benefits)[6] $__________
12. Plus equipment maintenance costs +$__________
13. Plus building maintenance costs +$__________
14. Plus other operating costs[7] +$__________

Equals total operating costs =$__________

Capital Costs (amortized)

15. Buildings[8] $__________
16. Plus baler and other processing equipment[9] +$__________
17. Plus other capital costs[10] +$__________

Equals total capital costs (amortized) =$__________

Total annual processing costs
(sum of operating and capital costs) =$__________(B)

---

[1] Include administrative costs.
[2] Include insurance, registration, fuel, lubricating fluids, parts, repairs.
[3] Such as supplies, miscellaneous hand tools, safety equipment and insurance.
[4] Such as plastics densification equipment.
[5] Include replacement costs and distribution costs.
[6] Include administrative costs.
[7] Such as supplies, miscellaneous hand tools, safety equipment, utilities, insurance and residue disposal costs.
[8] Include land, buildings, and site improvements, amortized over 20 years if owned, annual rental otherwise.
[9] Such as crushers, conveyors and separators.
[10] Such as scale, forklift other handling equipment.

SOURCE: How To Implement A Plastics Recycling Program, The Council for Solid Waste Solutions, 46-55.

APPENDIX C

(C) To Determine Transportation Costs:
Transportation costs for individual materials typically will be paid as a service fee to a trucking company or be "paid for" through a reduction in market price paid.

(D) To Determine Revenues:
For each collected material, multiply the annual tonnage anticipated by the expected market value per ton. (For plastics, see calculations on page 23.)

(E) To Determine Savings from Reduced Refuse Collection:
By diverting recyclables from the waste stream, there is less refuse requiring collection and subsequent transportation to the landfill or incinerator. Refuse collection trucks do not fill to capacity as quickly and can therefore remain on their routes longer and cover a greater number of stops (each having less refuse due to recycling) in a workday.

By removing difficult-to-compact recyclables such as plastics or corrugated cardboard, compaction is more efficient and allows for even higher tonnage collected per load. If fewer trucks and personnel are needed to collect refuse, credit can then be taken for any reduction in labor and/or equipment.

If the refuse and recyclable materials haulers are different organizations, savings will not be realized from reduced refuse collection. This is one of the reasons why it is so important to integrate collection of recyclables into the existing solid waste management system.

(F) To Determine the Savings from Reduced Refuse Disposal:
If disposal is performed under contract with a separate organization, fees will typically be assessed by cubic yard or ton. Credit should be taken for each unit (cubic yard or ton) which is diverted from the waste stream.

If Refuse Is Landfilled:
Determine how much each cubic yard of landfill space costs. Include the amortized capital costs of land; landfill development costs, and equipment (bulldozer, compactors) costs; estimated final closure of the landfill divided by the estimated lifetime capacity; post-closure costs; operating and maintenance costs (including labor, equipment, monitoring and environmental controls). Some organizations also include the "heirloom" costs (the loss of landfill property for future use).

Estimate the volume (cubic yards) of material diverted from the waste stream by recycling and multiply it by the total cost per cubic yard of the landfill.

18. Volume of material diverted from the waste stream (cubic yards) ____________

19. Multiplied by cost per cubic yard of the landfill x$____________

Equals the savings from reduced disposal =$____________(F)

RCE: How To Implement A Plastics Recycling Program, The Council for Solid Waste Solutions, 46-55.

If Refuse Is Incinerated:
Determine the tipping fee charged per ton at the incinerator. Estimate the tonnage of material diverted from the waste stream by recycling and multiply it by the total cost per ton charged by the incinerator operator.

20. Tonnage of material diverted from the waste stream ______

21. Multiplied by cost per ton of incineration x$______

Equals the savings from reduced disposal =$______(F)

Fully Allocated Costs of Various Recyclable Materials

Having now calculated total annual recycling system costs, the next step is to equitably allocate these costs among all of the recyclables collected. Slightly different approaches are required for commingled and separated material collection systems.

To determine what portion of the total recycling program costs should be allocated to the collection of each recyclable material (e.g., steel, aluminum, plastic, paper, glass) complete the following worksheets:

Commingled Material Collection

22. Annual collection costs $______(A)

23. Multiplied by the percent of the collection vehicle capacity devoted to (name of material) x______(G)

24. Equals the annual collection cost of (name of material) =$______

25. Plus cost to process (name of material) +$______(H)

26. Plus cost to transport (name of material) +$______

27. Minus revenue from the sale of (name of material) −$______

28. Minus the savings from reduced refuse collection −$______(E)

29. Minus the savings from reduced refuse disposal −$______(F)

Equals the net cost (savings) to recycle a particular recyclable material on an annual basis =$______

SOURCE: How To Implement A Plastics Recycling Program, The Council for Solid Waste Solutions, 46-55.

APPENDIX C

Source Separated Material and Curb Sort Collection

30. Collection equipment costs *(add lines 2 and 6)*	$________	
31. Multiplied by the percent of the collection vehicle capacity devoted to (name of material)	x________(G)	
32. Equals the collection equipment cost to be allocated to (name of material)		=$________
33. Plus the amortized cost of densification and/or storage equipment specifically for (name of material)[3] *(from line 7 or 9)*		+$________
34. Equals the total equipment cost allocated to (name of material)		=$________
35. Total annual collection labor costs *(from line 1)*	$________	
36. Multiplied by the percent of on-route collection time devoted to (name of material)	x________(I)	
37. Equals the labor cost allocated to (name of material)		=$________
38. Plus (name of material)'s share of fixed costs *(add lines 4, 5 and 8, then divide sum by total number of separated recyclable materials collected)*		+$________
39. Equals total collection cost for (name of material) *(add lines 34, 37 and 38)*		=$________
40. Plus the cost to process (name of material)		+$________(H)
41. Plus the cost to transport (name of material)		+$________
42. Minus the revenue from the sale of (name of material)		−$________
43. Minus the savings from reduced refuse collection		−$________(E)
44. Minus the savings from reduced refuse disposal		−$________(F)
Equals the net cost (savings) to recycle (name of material) on an annual basis		=$________

URCE: <u>How To Implement A Plastics Recycling Program</u>, The Council for Solid Waste Solutions, 46-55.

APPENDIX C

(G) To Determine What Percentage of the Usable Body Capacity of Curbside Recycling Collection Truck to Allocate to Each Recyclable Material:
Divide the space required to accommodate a particular material by the total usable capacity of the vehicle. For example, if an on-board plastics compactor occupies three cubic yards on a truck with a total usable capacity of 30 cubic yards, then 3 divided by 30 or 0.1 (10 percent) of the total truck costs should be allocated to plastic.

(H) To Estimate the Cost of Processing a Particular Material:
The cost of processing materials should be figured on a tonnage basis. (Processing facilities measure their flow-through in tons-per-hour or tons-per-day.)

45. Total procesing costs	$________(B)	
46. Minus all single material equipment costs[1]	−$________	
47. Minus total labor costs used for only one material[2]	−$________	
48. Equals the total shared processing costs		=$________
49. Multiplied by percent that (name of material) comprises of total annual tonnage processed	x________	
50. Equals (name of material)'s share of processing costs		=$________
51. Plus (name of material) equipment costs		+$________
52. Plus (name of material) labor costs		+$________
Equals total processing costs for (name of material)		=$________(H)

(I) To Estimate the Percentage of the Labor Cost on the Collection Route Devoted to the Collection and/or Separation of Each Recyclable:
It is useful to do a time study to determine the exact percent of time devoted to each recyclable material collected in any collection program.

Time studies of curbside sort systems that collect newspaper, flint glass, amber glass, green glass, tin, aluminum and mixed HDPE-PET plastics reveal that 12 percent of the collection time is devoted to plastic and 30 percent to glass. Thus, in this case, 12 percent and 30 percent of the total labor costs should be allocated to the collection of plastics and glass, respectively.

---
[1] Estimate the amortized cost for every piece of equipment devoted to one specific material, e.g., granulator for plastic, eddy current separator for aluminum, baler for paper, glass crusher, any single material conveyors.
[2] E.g., glass sorters, plastic sorters.

SOURCE: How To Implement A Plastics Recycling Program, The Council for Solid Waste Solutions, 46-55.

APPENDIX C

Sample Worksheets from Anytown U.S.A.

Collection

Anytown is a community of 48,000 people in the Midwest that recently implemented a multi-material curbside recycling program. Recyclables are picked up weekly at curbside where they are sorted by the collection truck driver. There are about 18,000 households in the town, and 65 percent of these households participate in the program each week.

Recyclable materials are collected in six 30-cubic-yard trucks, each with a single-person crew. The trucks cover 600 homes on their daily routes, making 390 stops per day. Each truck is equipped with a plastics compactor.

Material Collected	Pounds per Day *(per truck)*	Truck Capacity Used *(cubic yards)*
Aluminum	40	1.0
Clear glass	900	3.5
Green glass	300	1.0
Brown glass	200	0.5
HDPE & PET plastics	270	3.0
Newspaper	3,900	16.0
Steel cans	390	5.0
	6,000	30.0

Processing

Anytown's collection contractor processes 18 tons of recyclable material each day. This equates to 4,680 tons per year from Anytown's six collection routes. Glass is dumped directly from the collection trucks into roll-off boxes. All other materials are baled.

Material	Tons per Year
Aluminum	31.2
Glass	1,092.0
Newspaper	3,042.0
HDPE/PET (mixed)	210.6
Steel	304.2
Total materials handled	4,680.0

Transportation costs

All of Anytown's markets are one hour's drive from the processing facility and transportation costs are $100 per roundtrip.

Revenues

Calculations are based on prices quoted for the "East-Central" part of the country in the December 4, 1990 issue of *Recycling Times.*

Material	$ per Ton
Aluminum	610
Glass	15
Newspaper	15
HDPE/PET (mixed)	90
Steel	60

Savings from reduced refuse collection

Refuse collection costs in Anytown are $60 per ton ($24 per cubic yard). Typically, an efficient refuse collection organization will be able save 50 percent of its collection costs for each cubic yard of recyclable material it diverts from the refuse stream. Thus, a collection credit of $12 can be given for each compacted cubic yard of material collected as recyclables, rather than refuse.

JRCE: How To Implement A Plastics Recycling Program, The Council for Solid Waste Solutions, 46-55.

APPENDIX C

(A) To Determine the Annual Collection Costs: (per truck)

Operating Costs		
1. Labor (wages, taxes, benefits)[1]	$ 26,000	
2. Plus all vehicle operating/maintenance costs[2]	+$ 12,000	
3. Plus other collection/storage equipment (e.g., drop boxes) maintenance costs	+$ —	
4. Plus education/promotion costs	+$ 3,000	
5. Plus overhead and other operating costs[3]	+$ 15,000	
Equals total operating costs		=$ 56,000
Capital Costs (amortized)		
6. Collection trucks	$ 13,000	
7. Plus specialized equipment[4]	+$ 1,500	
8. Plus household set-out bins or bags[5]	+$ 2,500	
9. Plus storage containers (e.g., drop boxes)	+$ —	
10. Plus other capital costs	+$ 5,000	
Equals total capital costs (amortized)		=$ 22,000
Total annual collection costs *(sum of operating and capital costs)*		=$ 78,000 (A)

(B) To Determine the Annual Processing Costs:

Operating Costs		
11. Labor (wages, taxes, benefits)[6]	$ 54,000	
12. Plus equipment maintenance costs	+$ 10,000	
13. Plus building maintenance costs	+$ 3,000	
14. Plus other operating costs[7]	+$ 26,000	
Equals total operating costs		=$ 93,000
Capital Costs (amortized)		
15. Buildings[8]	$ 25,000	
16. Plus baler and other processing equipment[9]	+$ 13,000	
17. Plus other capital costs[10]	+$ 12,000	
Equals total capital costs (amortized)		=$ 50,000
Total annual processing costs *(sum of operating and capital costs)*		=$ 143,000 (B)

[1] Include administrative costs.
[2] Include insurance, registration, fuel, lubricating fluids, parts, repairs.
[3] Such as supplies, miscellaneous hand tools, safety equipment and insurance.
[4] Such as plastics densification equipment.
[5] Include replacement costs and distribution costs.
[6] Include administrative costs.
[7] Such as supplies, miscellaneous hand tools, safety equipment, utilities, insurance and residue disposal costs.
[8] Include land, buildings, and site improvements, amortized over 20 years if owned, annual rental otherwise.
[9] Such as crushers, conveyors and separators.
[10] Such as scale, forklift other handling equipment.

SOURCE: <u>How To Implement A Plastics Recycling Program</u>, The Council for Solid Waste Solutions, 46-55.

APPENDIX C

Source Separated Material and Curb Sort Collection

30. Collection equipment costs *(add lines 2 and 6)*	$25,000	
31. Multiplied by the percent of the collection vehicle capacity devoted to ~~(name of material)~~ plastic	x 10% (G)	
32. Equals the collection equipment cost to be allocated to ~~(name of material)~~ plastic		=$ 2,500
33. Plus the amortized cost of densification and/or storage equipment specifically for ~~(name of material)~~ plastic *(from line 7 or 9)*		+$ 1,500
34. Equals the total equipment cost allocated to ~~(name of material)~~ plastic		=$ 4,000
35. Total annual collection labor costs *(from line 1)*	$26,000	
36. Multiplied by the percent of on-route collection time devoted to ~~(name of material)~~ plastic	x 12% (I)	
37. Equals the labor cost allocated to ~~(name of material)~~ plastic		=$ 3,120
38. Plus ~~(name of material)~~ plastic's share of fixed costs *(add lines 4, 5 and 8, then divide sum by total number of separated recyclable materials collected)*		+$ 2,929
39. Equals total collection cost for ~~(name of material)~~ plastic *(add lines 34, 37 and 38)*		=$ 10,049
40. Plus the cost to process ~~(name of material)~~ plastic		+$ 1,430 (H)
41. Plus the cost to transport ~~(name of material)~~ plastic — 4 loads x $100/load		+$ 400
42. Minus the revenue from the sale of ~~(name of material)~~ plastic — 35.1 tons x $90/ton		-$ 3,159
43. Minus the savings from reduced refuse collection — $12/yd x 234 cubic yards of plastic recycled		-$ 2,808 (E)
44. Minus the savings from reduced refuse disposal — $50/ton x 35.1 tons		-$ 1,755 (F)
Equals the net cost (savings) to recycle (name of material) on an annual basis (per truck)		=$ 4,157

$4,157/35.1 tons = $118.43

CE: *How To Implement A Plastics Recycling Program*, The Council for Solid Waste Solutions, 46-55.

APPENDIX C

(H) To Estimate the Cost of Processing a Particular Material:
The cost of processing materials should be figured on a tonnage basis. (Processing facilities measure their flow-through in tons-per-hour or tons-per-day.)

45. Total processing costs	$ 143,000 (B)	
46. Minus all single material equipment costs[1]	−$ ______	
47. Minus total labor costs used for only one material[2]	−$ ______	
48. Equals the total shared processing costs		=$ 143,000
49. Multiplied by percent that ~~(name of material)~~ plastic comprises of total annual tonnage processed	x 6%	
50. Equals ~~(name of material)~~ plastic's share of processing costs		=$ 8,580
51. Plus (name of material) equipment costs		+$ ______
52. Plus (name of material) labor costs		+$ ______
Equals total processing costs for ~~(name of material)~~ – plastic		=$ 8,580 (H)

÷ 6 trucks = $1,430/truck

SOURCE: How To Implement A Plastics Recycling Program, The Council for Solid Waste Solutions, 46-55.

APPENDIX D

LANDFILL AND INCINERATOR DISPOSAL CAPACITY, NUMBERS, AND TIPPING FEES, BY STATE, 1989

State	Landfills			Incinerators		
	Number	Cost per Ton (dollars)	Remaining Capacity (no. of years)	Number	Cost per Ton (dollars)	Capacity (tons per day)
Alabama	107	$5.25	less than 4	1	n/a	225
Alaska	740	up to 40	15-20	2	up to $100	100
Arizona	100	up to 20	n/a	0		
Arkansas	85	15-20	less than 5	3	$20-30	160
California	423	3-30	10	3	15-20	2,500
Colorado	150	up to 45	n/a	0		
Connecticut	60	60-110	n/a	7	60-85	5,700
Delaware	3	42	20+	1	42	600
Dist. of Columbia	1	n/a	4	1	n/a	600
Florida	170	10-45	less than 5	10	45-65	9,200
Georgia	191	10-45	3-4	1	n/a	500
Hawaii	17	n/a	5	1	36	600
Idaho	110	up to 10	20	1	n/a	50
Illinois	126	8-29	7.5	1	n/a	1,200
Indiana	83	12	7-8	3	18	3,000
Iowa	82	10	11	1	37	125
Kansas	130	4-14	15-20	0		
Kentucky	83	6-20	5	0		
Louisiana	41	8-30	10+	0		
Maine	185	n/a	n/a	5	n/a	1,400
Maryland	41	up to 60	n/a	4	40-60	5,000
Massachusetts	160	45-65	6	10	45-65	8,600
Michigan	71	n/a	n/a	3	n/a	1,250
Minnesota	87	20-45	4-6	11	50-90	2,000
Mississippi	102	n/a	6	1	20	200
Missouri	84	13	9	3	n/a	50
Montana	140	15	10-20	1	50	70
Nebraska	39	6.50	8	0		
Nevada	150	up to 10	5-7	0		
New Hampshire	56	up to 50	5	17	n/a	910
New Jersey	90	70	n/a	1	n/a	400
New Mexico	130	n/a	2-5	0		
New York	250	50-120	10	12	50-120	9,877
North Carolina	124	up to 29	less than 5	2	n/a	250
North Dakota	70	n/a	n/a	0		
Ohio	103	15-20	5-10	7	15-20	3,750
Oklahoma	150	8-15	15	3	0-42	1,250
Oregon	94	26-50	20+	2	n/a	650
Pennsylvania	72	37	n/a	2	n/a	700
Rhode Island	4	13-59	2	0		
South Carolina	79	22	10	2	38	800
South Dakota	36	3-10	n/a	0		
Tennessee	110	n/a	n/a	4	n/a	1,450
Texas	934	8-13	15	8	n/a	200
Utah	40	up to 20	20+	1	35	350
Vermont	60	10-75	n/a	0		
Virginia	257	15	n/a	7	35	4,000
Washington	95	35	20+	4	75	370
West Virginia	51	15	2	0		
Wisconsin	700+	n/a	n/a	8	n/a	1,300
Wyoming	113	10-12	20+	0		
TOTAL	7,379			154		

n/a: Figure not available.

JRCE: Solid Waste Management: Planning Issues and Opportunities (1990), 15.

APPENDIX E

AVERAGE RESALE VALUES OF RECYCLEABLES BY REGION

Recent average market prices for recyclables

(Prices per ton and by region)

	Northeast	East	Midwest	South	West
Old newspapers	$10–25	$10–20	$10–20	$0–25	$30–40
Mixed waste paper	$(-)10–10*	$0–75	$0–5	$(-)10*	$10–12
Aluminum cans	$600–900	$540–800	$600–900	$700–900	$500–780
Steel cans	$70	$110	$50–70	$50–80	$20–70
Plastic soft-drink containers (clear)	$180	$200	$170	$100	$140
Plastic milk jugs (clear)	$100 to 160	$140–200	$200	$100–200	$100–200

* Negative dollar amount indicates sum paid to have recyclable material hauled away.

Sources: Industry estimates, National Solid Wastes Management Association, Washington

Graphic by Kimberly Mart

SOURCE: Todd Sloane, "To Market, to Market." *City and State* (January 28, 1991), 14.

Printed in the USA
CPSIA information can be obtained
at www.ICGtesting.com
LVHW010440030124
767910LV00019B/1351

9 784094 656220